j932 Kap

Politics and Government
IN ANCIENT EGYPT

Leslie C. Kaplan

The Rosen Publishing Group's
PowerKids Press™
PRIMARY SOURCE

New York

To Melinda Shapiro

Published in 2004 by The Rosen Publishing Group, Inc.
29 East 21st Street, New York, NY 10010

First Edition

Editor: Joanne Randolph
Book Design: Maria E. Melendez
Photo Researcher: Adriana Skura

Photo Credits: Cover and p. 8 © Werner Forman/Art Resource, NY; cover (inset), pp. 7 (inset), 8 (inset), 11, 12 © Erich Lessing/Art Resource, NY; p. 4 © Michael Maslan Historic Photographs/CORBIS; pp. 7, 19 The Art Archive/Egyptian Museum Cairo/Dagli Orti; p. 12 (inset) © Scala/Art Resource, NY; p. 15 The Granger Collection, New York; p 15 (inset) © Charles & Josette Lenars/CORBIS; p. 16 The Art Archive/Bibliotheque des Arts Decoratifs Paris/Dagli Orti; p. 19 (inset) The Art Archive/Egyptian Museum Cairo; p. 20 The Art Archive/Dagli Orti.

Kaplan, Leslie C.
   Politics and government in ancient Egypt / Leslie C. Kaplan.—1st ed.
     p. cm.— (Primary sources of ancient civilizations. Egypt)
   Includes bibliographical references and index.
Contents: The king of ancient Egypt—One king after another—The second in command—How the power was divided —Priests and scribes—Laws and rights—Crime and punishment—The Egyptian army—The Egyptian navy—Life at the top.
   ISBN 0-8239-6783-2 (library binding)—ISBN 0-8239-8933-X (pbk.)
1. Egypt—Politics and government—To 332 B.C.—Juvenile literature.   [1. Egypt—Politics and government—To 332 B.C.] I. Title. II. Series.
   DT83.K26 2004
   320.932—dc21   2002151550

Manufactured in the United States of America

Contents

Egypt was divided into two kingdoms until 3100 B.C. These were Lower Egypt, or the Red Land, and Upper Egypt, or the White Land. Lower Egypt, in blue and yellow on the map, was to the north. It was called Lower Egypt because the Nile ran from south to north. Upper Egypt is shown in brown.

In the Beginning

Ancient Egypt existed between 3100 B.C. and 332 B.C. The politics and government of Egypt changed a great deal over this time. Before 3400 B.C., Egypt was occupied by separate groups of people. Each group ruled with its own king and worshiped its own gods. Over time these groups joined to form nomes, or districts. By 3400 B.C., Egypt consisted of two kingdoms, which were united in 3100 B.C. After 3100 B.C., historians talk about Egypt in terms of dynasties, or powerful families that rule a place for a long time. There were 31 major dynasties before Greece conquered Egypt in 332 B.C. A dynasty changed when someone seized power from the current king.

The King of Ancient Egypt

Kings, or pharaohs, ruled ancient Egypt between 3100 B.C. and 332 B.C. The Egyptians believed that each ruler was the powerful god Horus, son of the Sun God Re, in a human body. They thought that the king controlled everything in ancient Egypt, including the Sun and the Nile River. He controlled the temples, the army, the economy, and trade. He oversaw all government officials. The king owned most of the land in Egypt. Menes was the first king to rule all of Egypt. In about 3100 B.C., he united Egypt's two kingdoms, the Red Land and the White Land. Menes set up a capital in the city of Memphis and formed the world's first national government.

King Tutankhamen was Egypt's king between 1361 and 1352 B.C. Egyptians called their rulers pharaohs. "Pharaoh" means "great house."

In this carving, Menes, also called Narmer, is shown wearing the White Crown as he conquers Lower Egypt. Menes was a king in southern, or Upper, Egypt before he united the two districts.

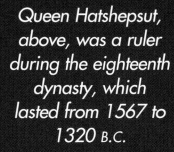

Queen Hatshepsut, above, was a ruler during the eighteenth dynasty, which lasted from 1567 to 1320 B.C.

Great Royal Wife Nefertiti is shown with her husband Akhenaton and three of their six daughters. Nefertiti played an important political and religious role in the cult that worshiped the god of Aton, the Sun disk. She is shown in tomb paintings as an equal partner to her husband.

The Great Royal Wife

Kings had many wives at once. However, only one wife held the title of Great Royal Wife. It was through her that the royal line was passed down. Egyptians had less confidence in kings not born of the Great Royal Wife. Her oldest daughter, the Great Royal Daughter, would become the next Great Royal Wife. Her oldest son inherited the throne by marrying the daughter at the king's death. Though the Great Royal Wife always had a lot of power, she rarely ruled Egypt. Hatshepsut crowned herself ruler when her stepson, the future king, was a baby. She ruled from 1503 to 1482 B.C. Her stepson disliked her for taking power and might have killed Hatshepsut to become king.

The Second in Command

The king often chose a close friend or a relative to be his second in command. This person's title was vizier. He served as the king's eyes and ears. A vizier needed to be aware of what was happening in Egypt. He controlled the water and food supplies. He also hired lower government officials, kept public records, and mobilized troops in case of war. The vizier's job was so hard that the king often appointed two. Between 1570 and 1069 B.C., for example, the kings used two viziers. One oversaw the activities in the Nile delta area and lived in Memphis. The other took care of the region of Upper Egypt to the south and lived in Thebes.

Rekhmire, the vizier of kings Thutmose III and Amenhotep II, inspects the work of goldsmiths. The vizier had many important tasks, including serving as a tax collector and an important judge.

These writing tools were used by Egyptian scribes around the mid-1300s B.C.

Scribes used reed pens and paper made from the papyrus plant to record information such as the size of the harvest, as this wall painting shows.

How the Power Was Divided

The government of ancient Egypt had the structure of a pyramid. The king ruled at the top. Beneath him was a hierarchy of workers. Only a few people held positions of great power. These were the king's chief officers, who included the vizier and the high priest. These men oversaw lower officials in areas such as law, religion, agriculture, and trade. Judges, priests, scribes, and nobles played key roles in government. Lower in the hierarchy, there was a large group of officials who oversaw all the farmers, the craftsmen, and the soldiers. However indirectly, all officials obeyed the orders of the king, whose word was law.

Laws and Rights

Egyptian law was based on the religious belief in Ma'at. Ma'at was the goddess of truth, justice, and balance. Each king and his government created laws to make sure that people followed these ideals. Many laws were designed to protect and provide for people after death. There were also many laws to protect the family. Men and women had nearly equal rights in ancient Egypt. Both could own property and sue others, and both could have jobs, though most women ran their households. Women kept lawful right to their own property in a marriage. Slaves were the lowest members of society and had the fewest rights. They could own property, though.

Above: *Slaves serve women at a banquet. Slaves could be freed by their owners, but until then slaves had few rights.*

Ma'at, the goddess of order and justice, stands beside her father Re, the Sun God.

These prisoners are building a temple in Thebes. Some criminals
had to leave their families to go to work in mines in the desert.
Punished criminals lived in shame. They
could regain their social standing only by
performing some brave act.

Crime and Punishment

People who broke the law in ancient Egypt got punished. The local police had the job of catching criminals. Courts decided how criminals should be punished. There were two kinds of courts in ancient Egypt. One was the local court, or *kenbet*, which handled most cases. The other was the High Court, located in the capital. This court handled serious crimes. The vizier headed the court system. Judges tried to keep citizens from misbehaving by making examples of the criminals. Beatings with sticks were common. Criminals who tried to escape got their nose or ears cut off. A person could be killed for serious crimes, such as plotting to harm the king.

The Egyptian Army

At first ancient Egyptian rulers had no paid army. They relied on volunteers. Egypt had good natural resources and rarely attacked other lands. Then, around 1675 B.C., the Hyksos, who lived across the Sinai Peninsula, took control of Egypt. The Egyptians finally regained control around 1567 B.C. Decades of war had created experienced Egyptian soldiers. Egypt's strong army conquered lands such as Syria and Palestine, and the empire grew. Soldiers took slaves, jewels, ivory, and metals from the people they conquered. Kings personally led the armies into battles. Temple scenes showed kings single-handedly defeating enemies on behalf of the gods.

These models of Egyptian soldiers were created around 2000 B.C., during the Eleventh Dynasty.

The Hyksos introduced the Egyptians to new battle methods and weapons. They also introduced the chariot. This was an open, two-wheeled cart, in which two men stood. One man drove the two horses that pulled the chariot. The other man fought.

Ships are being built in a shipyard in Saqqara, Egypt. This scene was painted between 2446 and 2426 B.C., during the Fifth Dynasty. The bigger ships were up to 200 feet (61 m) long.

Ancient Egypt was one of the first civilizations to have a navy. The Egyptians built a fleet of ships to protect the Mediterranean coast from invaders. The navy's main job was to carry soldiers and supplies. Soldiers were also trained to board enemy ships and to fight at sea. A famous sea battle took place under the rule of Ramses III. Around 1200 B.C., his coasts were in danger from the Sea Peoples, invaders from the Mediterranean. He used his navy to trap and destroy the Sea Peoples' fleet. The activity of the military reflected Egypt's foreign policy. During some dynasties, Egypt invaded more lands. In others the kings worked to form peaceful relationships with neighbors.

Life at the Top

Governments ideally appoint their officials based on merit. In ancient Egypt, many top government positions were hereditary. This means that viziers, nobles, and priests passed their jobs to their sons. The king paid them with big estates, fancy tombs, and gold. The goods and services of merchants, artists, and farmers were used to benefit the elite. People usually married within their own class. This made it hard for the lower classes to move up in society. It may seem unfair that a few lived in luxury while most did not. However, the class system provided order in society and helped the Egyptian civilization to flourish for centuries.

Glossary

agriculture (A-grih-kul-cher) The science of producing crops and raising livestock, or animals.

delta (DEL-tuh) A pile of earth and sand that collects at the mouth of a river.

elite (ay-LEET) A small, powerful group of people.

fleet (FLEET) Many ships under the command of one person.

hierarchy (HY-rar-kee) A ruling body arranged by rank or class.

inherited (in-HEHR-it-ed) To have received something after the former owner died.

invaders (in-VAYD-erz) People who enter a place in order to attack and conquer.

mobilized (MOH-buh-lyzd) To have gathered and made ready for action.

policy (PAH-lih-see) A law that people use to help them make decisions.

pyramid (PEER-uh-mid) A huge structure that held the grave of an Egyptian ruler, called a pharaoh.

scribes (SKRYBZ) People whose job is to copy books by hand.

stepson (STEP-sun) A son of one's husband or wife by another marriage.

sue (SOO) To seek justice from a person by taking legal action.

tomb (TOOM) Grave.

Index

Primary Sources

Cover. Queen Hatshepsut is shown as a male pharaoh with Seshat, the writing goddess, in a foundation ceremony. Relief. Red Chapel of Hatshepsut. Deir el-Bahari, Egypt. Circa 1479–1458 B.C.. **Inset.** May, the royal scribe and keeper of the treasure. Limestone. Circa 1350 B.C. Rijkmuseum van Oudheden. Leiden, Netherlands. **Page 4.** 1826 map of Egypt. Joseph Perkins. **Page 7.** King Tutankhamen anointed with his wife Ankhsenamun. Detail of the back of King Tutankhamen's throne. Gold and inlay. Tomb of King Tutankhamen. Circa 1336–1327 B.C.. Egyptian Museum, Cairo, Egypt. **Inset.** The Narmer Palette. One side of the two-sided palette. On this side Menes is wearing the White Crown as he subdues Lower Egypt. On the reverse he wears the Red Crown symbolizing his unification of Egypt. **Page 8.** Akhenaton, Nefertiti, and their 3 daughters sit beneath the rays of Aton, the Sun. Stela relief. Circa 1352–1336 B.C. Egyptian Museum, Cairo. **Inset.** Queen Hatshepsut seated. Pink granite. Circa 1479–1458 B.C. Rijkmuseum van Oudheden. Leiden, Netherlands. **Page 11.** Rekhmire, vizier to kings Thutmose III and Amenophis II, inspects the work of his goldsmiths. Detail of wallpainting. Tomb of Rekhmire. Cemetery of the Sheik Abd el-Qurna. Tomb of the Nobles. Thebes, Egypt. **Page 12.** Scribes with reed pens and papyrus sheets are measuring and recording the harvest. Detail of wallpainting. Tomb of Mennah, scribe of the fields and estate inspector to pharaoh Thutmose IV. Circa 1500–1300 B.C. Cemetery of the Sheik Abd el-Qurna. **Inset.** Scribe palettes. Schist.From Tell al-Ruba (Mendes). Egyptian Museum. Cairo. **Page 15.** Maid servants attending ladies at a banquet. Fresco. Tomb of Vizier Rekhmire. Eighteenth Dynasty. **Inset.** God Re and his daughter Ma'at. painting. Tomb of Queen Taousert. **Page 16.** Prisoners building a temple to Amun. 1878 engraving based on a fresco from the Eighteenth Dynasty in Thebes, Egypt. **Page 19.** Egyptian Pikemen. Wooden model figures. Tomb of Mesehti. Circa 2000 B.C. Egyptian Museum, Cairo. **Inset.** Gold Chariot of King Tutankhamen. Egyptian Museum. Cairo. **Page 20.** Shipbuilding in a shipyard. Bas-relief. Tomb of Ti, an official servant under Pharaoh Kakai. Circa 2446–2426 B.C. Saqqara, Egypt.

Web Sites

Due to the changing nature of Internet links, PowerKids Press has developed an online list of Web sites related to the subject of this book. This site is updated regularly. Please use this link to access the list:
www.powerkidslinks.com/psaciv/poliegy/